PRAYER:
A FIELD GUIDE

PRAYER:
A FIELD GUIDE

Fr. Charles H. Nalls, SSM

iUniverse, Inc.
New York Bloomington

Prayer: A Field Guide

iUniverse books may be ordered through booksellers or by contacting:

iUniverse
1663 Liberty Drive
Bloomington, IN 47403
www.iuniverse.com
1-800-Authors (1-800-288-4677)

Because of the dynamic nature of the Internet, any Web addresses or links contained in this book may have changed since publication and may no longer be valid.

The views expressed in this work are solely those of the author and do not necessarily reflect the views of the publisher, and the publisher hereby disclaims any responsibility for them.

ISBN: 978-0-595-49142-1 (pbk)
ISBN: 978-0-595-60982-6 (ebk)

Printed in the United States of America

For our young people, especially Laura

"Prayer needs no teacher. It requires diligence, effort and personal ardor, and then God will be its teacher."

—*St. Meletius the Confessor*

Contents

ACKNOWLEDGMENTS

I make no pretense that this is an "original" or complete work. The first version was rushed to print in 2003 for the Good Shepherd Youth Camp, where it made its debut. I have borrowed extensively from the Fathers of the Church and their thoughts on prayer, as well as a number of writers who have done a far better job with this topic than I. As well, there are many other people who have provided inspiration, ideas, assistance, and criticism for this book. In particular, Jeanmarie Keeney, an outstanding teacher, catechist, and editor, has given generously of her time and talent to make this book possible.

I am very fortunate to have had as a personal mentor and dear friend a fine priest and scholar, the Very Rev. David F. T. Rodier, lately retired from the Department of Philosophy and Religion at the American University. His patience, unstinting generosity with his time and knowledge of the faith continue to support my efforts as a priest and sometime writer.

I also owe much inspiration in the revision of this book to my good friend Chaplain (Colonel) William Sean Lee of the Maryland National Guard. Chaplain Lee truly is a man whose "habit of prayer" allows him to draw others into conversation with God in times of great joy and moments of the deepest sorrow. Here is a man who helps teach others to "pray aright."

I am indebted to so many others for the encouragement they have given me as a priest and in the preparation of this book, I would be very remiss if I did not thank my friends and teachers at the Dominican House of Studies in Washington, D.C., and those whom I am privileged to serve—the men and women of the 70th Regiment (LDR), Maryland National Guard, who give to this chaplain much more than he can ever give to them and the people of St. Athanasius Mission, Glen Allen, Virginia, steadfast in faith.

My special debt for this work, though, lies with Bishop Rocco A. Florenza, a true pastor whose prayer life and work for the unity of Christ's Church is an example to his clergy, and with the Benedictines of St. Anselm's Abbey in Washington, D.C. St. Anselm's is a community that truly prays throughout each day, and the Benedictine example of prayer shines forth in a benighted world. St. Benedict has taught me to "pray into the interstices of the day," to try to fill each otherwise wasted or idle moment with a prayer offering of some sort. I have to say that I am a long way from there, but, in the words of the old Gospel song, I'm "working on the building ..."

Finally, as always, to Our Lady of Walsingham, may she never cease her intercession for us all.

Trinitytide 2008   CHN+

PREFACE
TO THE 2008 EDITION

There are a number of books on prayer—there seem to be as many as there are grains of sand on the beach. Some are short; some are not so short. Many are very, very good, and I have included some of my favorites in the Suggested Reading and Resources section. So, with all of these materials on the market, why write another book on prayer?

First, there are so many genuinely bad basic books on the topic—books that are neither good nor useful. Many are little more than thinly disguised New Age tracts. In these books, the "mantra" of repeated phrases takes the place of authentic prayer. These are dangerously misleading works that we are wise to avoid.

Secondly, there is a class of material I like to call "gimmee" prayers. These teach a sort of bartering with God in which a person can get what they want just by asking the right way. These books promise health, wealth, recovery, love, and so on if one approaches God according to the formula set out by the writer. These, too, are a spiritual blight and lead to damage to faith when God's plan might be something other than that of the individual offering the prayer.

Finally, I wanted to provide a short pamphlet for teenagers and young adults who are learning to pray, asking why they should pray, or asking why we traditional Catholic and Anglican folk pray the way we do. On this last point, there is a wonderful pattern of regular prayers that we find in the Book of Common Prayer, either the American 1928 edition or the English book of 1662, the Breviary, and the Liturgy of the Hours. As well, there are hundreds of little devotionals incorporating these and similar prayers.

For those used to "free form" prayer, particularly young people, these prayers can at first seem a bit stiff and formal. Yet, they are words of prayer to have at hand when you cannot think of anything to say to God—familiar words that stand on their own or which allow one to move quickly into more complex and more contemplative prayers. This little book also talks about these deeper forms of prayer once the "training wheels" come off.

At the end of the day, we Christians believe in the need for and power of prayer—our Lord Jesus Christ teaches us that it is our way of life. We want this life and particularly want our children to have this life. Yet, we often have little or nothing to offer to our children other than to have them say grace over a meal or the Lord's Prayer. These are good things, but we need more—to have a "prayer life." I have put this booklet together to help in that effort.

The Rev. Charles Hart Nalls
Washington, D.C.
June 2008

✝

CHAPTER I

WHAT IS PRAYER?

I have called this book *Prayer: A Field Guide*. Why this "field guide" label? Well, field guides provide short answers to practical questions. They are handy references for basic situations you find in everyday life. For instance, the field books used by our armed forces, Scouts, and outdoor enthusiasts throughout the world give basic definitions and guidance on everything from picking out a good place to camp, first aid, and how to cook, to ways to identify plants and animals. These books are mostly guides for survival in the wilderness. They are the "how-to" manuals for taking care of your basic needs in tough situations.

This is what this little book is designed to do. It is meant to be a pocket survival guide for the world; for prayer is the means of survival for you as a Christian. Prayer is first aid for a hurting soul, food for a hungry spirit, and safe rest for you when you are lost in unfamiliar country.

Effects of Prayer

Prayer can change the world. It can have great and immediate effects such as healing or a gift of peace to a troubled heart. In hearing our prayers,

God does not change his will or action in our regard, but simply puts into effect what he had eternally decreed in view of our prayer. Our Lord may do this directly as when he gives to us as individuals some supernatural gift, such as actual grace. Here, we can receive strength to deal with a situation that is far beyond our own control. Or God may answer our prayers indirectly, when he bestows some natural gift. In this second case, his providence directs natural causes, such as people who contribute to what we are praying for such as, for example, physicians who heal the sick. Finally, by miraculous intervention, and without using us or anyone else, he can produce the effect prayed for.

Let's look at scripture, for the Bible reveals how prayers are answered.

How Are Prayers Answered?

IMMEDIATELY AT TIMES—"Before they call I will answer, while they are yet speaking I will hear" (Isaiah 65:24).

Or

"[W]hile I was speaking in prayer, the man Gabriel, whom I had seen in the vision at the first, came to me in swift flight at the time of the evening sacrifice. He came and he said to me, 'O Daniel, I have now come out to give you wisdom and understanding. At the beginning of your supplications a word went forth, and I have come to tell it to you, for you are greatly beloved; therefore consider the word and understand the vision'" (Daniel 9:21–23).

DELAYED AT TIMES—"And will not God vindicate his elect, who cry to him day and night? Will he delay long over them?" (Luke 18:7).

DIFFERENT FROM OUR DESIRES—"Three times I besought the Lord about this, that it should leave me; but he said to me, 'My grace is sufficient for you, for my power is made perfect in weakness.' I will all the more gladly boast of my weaknesses, that the power of Christ may rest upon me" (II Corinthians 12:8–9).

BEYOND OUR EXPECTATIONS—"Call to me and I will answer you, and will tell you great and hidden things which you have not known" (Jeremiah 33:3).

Or

"Now to him who by the power at work within us is able to do far more abundantly than all that we ask or think" (Ephesians 3:20).

The very use of prayer, or habit of prayer, benefits us in many ways. Besides obtaining the gifts and graces we need, the process of prayer raises our minds and hearts to a knowledge and love of the divine and gives us greater confidence in God. These are great things, whether we act with a gift from God in answer to our prayers or others act as a result of our prayers or when God himself directly answers prayers.

But what is it that we are doing when we pray? First, let's look at what prayer is and isn't.

What Prayer Is

Prayer is an act of the virtue of religion which consists in asking proper gifts or graces from God. In a more general sense, it is the application of the mind to divine things, not merely to acquire a knowledge of them but to make use of such knowledge as a means of union with God. We can do this by acts of praise and thanksgiving, but petition is the principal act of prayer.

In scripture, the words used to describe prayer are:

To call up (Genesis 4:26)

To intercede (Job 23:10)

To mediate (Isaiah 53:10)

To consult (I Kings 28:6)

To beseech (Exodus 33:11)

To cry out to (there are many examples in the Psalms alone!)

The Fathers of the Church speak of it as the elevation of the mind to God with a view to asking proper things from him (St. John Damascene), communing and conversing with God (St. Gregory of Nyssa), and talking with God (St. John Chrysostom). It is therefore the expression of our desires to God whether for ourselves or others.

This expression of our desires is not intended to instruct or direct God in what to do but to appeal to his goodness for the things we need. The appeal is necessary, not because he is ignorant of our needs or sentiments, but to give definite form to our desires, to concentrate our whole attention on what we have to recommend to him, and to help us appreciate our close, personal relation with him. Our appeal need not always be external or vocal; it is sufficient if our prayer is internal or mental.

PRAYER IS COMMUNICATING WITH GOD
It takes different forms, but essentially, it occurs when man talks with God and God talks with man. Prayer is also:

- Calling upon the name of the Lord (Genesis 12:8)
- Crying unto God (Psalms 27:7; 34:6)
- Drawing near to God (Psalm 73:28; Hebrews 10:22)
- Looking up (Psalm 5:3)
- Lifting up the soul (Psalm 25:1)
- Lifting up the heart (Lamentations 3:41)
- Pouring out the heart (Psalm 62:8)
- Pouring out the soul (I Samuel 1:15)
- Crying to Heaven (II Chronicles 32:20)
- Beseeching the Lord (Exodus 32:11)
- Seeking God (Job 8:5)
- Seeking the face of the Lord (Psalm 27:8)
- Making supplication (Job 8:5; Jeremiah 36:7)

Look at the type of communication—it always is active. We beseech, cry, seek, call, lift up, and pour out.

PRAYER IS CONVERSATION AND A ONE-WAY CONVERSATION DOES NOT LAST LONG
When you pray, expect God to speak to you. He may do this through his written word or by a "still small voice" that seems to "speak" to your heart.

Just remember that this dialogue with God, who does not speak as we do, differs from an ordinary conversation. It is an interior light, a heart-to-heart intimacy whose fruit is sentiments of gratitude, humility, contrition, or perhaps resolution.

The definition given by St. John Damascene, "To pray is to offer one's heart to God," conveys this attitude of soul. On the other hand, to define prayer as "dialoguing with God" (St. Augustine), "raising one's heart to God" (St. Gregory of Nyssa), "friendly conversation with God" (St. Teresa of Avila) is to have grasped the obvious aspects of prayer.

An opposite definition of prayer would be "to be silent" and "to submerge one's soul in God." Carrying the concept further, it would be better to say that not only the soul but also the body is submerged in God. Finally, there is a wonderful saying that, "The end of prayer is to be snatched away to God" (St. Gregory Palamas, Triads II.iii.35).

Prayer is powerful, particularly when all of us in our Christian community are praying together. We know from the example of St. Peter in prison that the prayer of Christians in community makes chains fall away, opens the prison doors, and calls the angels down from heaven in reply. But there are many misunderstandings about prayer that can confuse us or lead to disappointment because we don't really know what we are doing when we pray. That is why it is important to know what prayer is not.

What Prayer Is Not

There are thousands and thousands of books written about prayer. Many of these claim that certain prayers are guaranteed to bring you wealth or love or improvement in life. A large number of these base their claims on reciting the right "formula" or repeated phrase. These claims are simply wrong.

Here is what prayer is not:

- Praying is not merely repeating the words of prayers.
- Prayer isn't magic.
- Prayer isn't a "gimmee" or swap of devotion for something you want.
- Prayer isn't bargaining with God.
- Prayer is not just talking to God; it *involves listening* also.

To pray does not mean to tire yourself out thinking about God. It is, rather, to rest your heart in God and hear what he is saying to you. This does not mean that the sufferings of everyday life just go away or that we will receive what we want. We pray as human beings for whom life's problems are not only inevitable, but often intensified during those moments when they weigh on us. A large part of the difficulty comes when we don't know what to pray for. If we don't know the proper object of prayer, then we may not actually be praying.

What Should We Pray For?

First: We should pray that the number one passion in our lives is seeking and carrying out God's will as we are able to discern it. *"Incline my heart according to your will, O God"* is a prayer from the Liturgy of the Hours that should be always on our lips.

Second: We should pray that we discover and become the unique person God has created us to be. Two lines from a prayer that express this best say:

Give me the freedom to grow that I may

become my true self,

the fulfillment of the seed which you

planted in me at my making.

Too often, we waste time trying to be someone we are not. Reflective prayer can help us to distinguish our true self from our false self.

Third: Since all of us have a particular vocation in life (married, single, religious) and most of us have either our studies in school or a particular career with duties, we should often pray that God will help us to be faithful to our studies, our vocation, and our duties in life.

Fourth: We should often pray for our own continuing conversion.

Fifth: We should talk to God about the nitty-gritty stuff of our daily lives: a particular ailment, a cross we are carrying, a relationship, a career choice, whether something will hurt our relationship with God or family, and so on.

The Problem of "Unanswered" Prayers

Here is the major question for many Christians: Why does God seem not to answer some of our prayers? Few things can hurt our relationship with God more than the feeling that he is deaf to our prayers, especially to concerns that are very important to us. There are lots of reasons why God may not answer our prayers in the way we want. The following are some of them:

- We ask without forgiveness. "And whenever you stand praying, forgive, if you have anything against anyone; so that your Father also who is in heaven may forgive you your trespasses" (St. Mark 11:25).

- We ask wrongly. "You ask and do not receive, because you ask wrongly, to spend it on your passions" (St. James 4:3).

- We lack faith and persistence. "Therefore I tell you, whatever you ask in prayer, believe that you have received it, and it will be yours" (St. Mark 11:24); "For everyone who asks receives, and he who seeks finds, and to him who knocks it will be opened" (St. Luke 11:10).

- We fail to do our own part. "Thus Hezekiah did throughout all Judah; and he did what was good and right and faithful before the LORD his God" (II Chronicles 31:20).

We may pray for success in an exam, but we fail to study. We pray for reconciliation of a hurt, but we do nothing to heal the conflict.

God may not answer our prayers as we would like him to, because "God's ways are not our ways" (Isaiah 55:8). Here are two examples: Jesus in Gethsemane and St. Paul's "thorn in the flesh" (II Corinthians 12:7–10).

You know, God may also just give us the simple answer "No." Part of listening to God is hearing the answer that we might not want to hear. Remember, we must always pray that it is God's will that should be done—not ours.

Prayer and Distraction

I would like to say something about "background noise" and its effect on prayer. At times, prayer can be so filled with distractions that we can no longer discern that we are praying. If you give in to distraction, then you are not praying, even though you may be saying the words. Yet at precisely such times, prayer becomes knowing how to submerge body and soul in God while sinking up to our necks or over our heads in life's troubles.

At this point, our troubles can even be converted into "food for prayer." When we confess, "I can no longer pray," then prayer becomes God's work rather than our own effort. When we cry out with sorrow and desire, "I cannot love; help me to love," then God's love, not ours, becomes active.

When we find that we can't pray, can't love, can't find intimate friend-ship with God, and can't raise our hearts to God or even converse with him, the regular definitions of prayer will not help at all. Only through letting go of active prayer will we be able to reach for the true prayer of prayers. Then we simply say, "Lord, I can't pray right now. Please pray in me."

"Likewise the Spirit helps us in our weakness; for we do not know how to pray as we ought, but the Spirit intercedes with sighs too deep for words" (Romans 8:26).

And just remember:

Don't bother talking to God ... unless you are willing to listen to him.

CHAPTER II

WHY PRAY?

Many people today do not see the need for regular, formal prayer. "I pray when I feel moved to, when it is meaningful to me," they say. People with this attitude overlook two important things: the purpose of prayer and the need for practice.

One purpose of prayer is to increase your awareness of God and the role that he plays in your life. If you only pray when you feel inspired or "moved" to (that is, when you are already aware of God), then you will not increase your awareness of God. You won't be growing in your faith.

In addition, if you want to do something well, you have to practice it continually, even when you don't feel like doing it. This is as true of prayer as it is of playing a sport, playing a musical instrument, or writing.

The sense of humility and awe of God that is essential to proper prayer does not come easily to modern man, and it will not simply come to you when you feel the need to pray. If you wait until inspiration strikes, you will not have the skills you need to pray effectively.

Before I started praying regularly, I found that when I wanted to pray, I didn't know how. I didn't know what to say, or how to say it, or how to establish the proper frame of mind. When you pray regularly, you will learn how to express yourself in prayer.

By prayer, we acknowledge God's power and goodness and our own neediness and dependence. It is therefore an act of the virtue of religion implying the deepest reverence for God. It trains us to look to him for everything, not merely because the thing we ask may be good in itself or advantageous to us but chiefly because we wish it as a gift of God. Prayer presupposes faith in God and hope in his goodness. By both, God, to whom we pray, moves us to prayer.

Our knowledge of God by the light of our own natural reason may inspire us to look to him for help, but such prayer lacks supernatural inspiration. Though such prayer may help to keep us from losing our natural knowledge of God and trust in him, or, to some extent, from offending him, it cannot really prepare us to receive his incredible graces and gifts.

Necessity of Prayer

Prayer is necessary for salvation, and it is a distinct precept of Christ in the Gospels. The precept imposes on us only what is really necessary for salvation. Here are some examples for you to use:

ST. MATTHEW 6:9—"Pray then like this: Our Father who art in heaven, Hallowed be thy name ..." (You know the rest!)

ST. MATTHEW 7:7—"Ask, and it will be given you; seek, and you will find; knock, and it will be opened to you."

ST. LUKE 11:9—"And I tell you, Ask, and it will be given you; seek, and you will find; knock, and it will be opened to you."

ST. JOHN 16:26—"In that day you will ask in my name ..."

COLOSSIANS 4:2—"Continue steadfastly in prayer, being watchful in it with thanksgiving ..."

ROMANS 12:12—"Rejoice in your hope, be patient in tribulation, be constant in prayer."

I PETER 4:7—"The end of all things is at hand; therefore keep sane and sober for your prayers."

Without prayer, we cannot resist temptation, cannot obtain God's grace, cannot grow and persevere in the Christian life. This need is common to everyone according to their different states in life, especially to priests, for instance, or to those with special religious obligations, who, in a special manner, pray for their own welfare and for the good of others.

The obligation to pray is incumbent on us at all times. "And he spoke also a parable to them that we ought always to pray, and not to faint" (St. Luke 15:1). This obligation is especially pressing when we are in great need of prayer, when without it, we cannot overcome some obstacle or perform some obligation; when, to fulfill various obligations of charity, we should pray for others; and when it is specially implied in some obligation, such as attendance at Mass and the observance of Sundays and feast days. This is true of vocal prayer, and as regards mental prayer, or meditation, this, too, is necessary insofar as we may need to apply our mind to the study of divine things in order to acquire a knowledge of the truths necessary for salvation.

The obligation to pray is upon us at all times, not that prayer should be our sole occupation. The texts of scripture telling us to pray without ceasing mean that we must pray whenever it is necessary, as it so frequently is necessary that we must continue to pray until we shall have obtained what we need.

Some writers speak of a virtuous life as an uninterrupted prayer and appeal to the adage "to toil is to pray." This does not mean that virtue or work replaces the duty of prayer, since it is not possible either to practice virtue or to work properly without frequent use of prayer.

The practice of the Church, devoutly followed by the faithful, is to begin and end the day with prayer, and though morning and evening prayer is not of strict obligation, the practice of it so well satisfies our sense of the need of prayer that neglect of it, especially for a long time, is regarded as more or less sinful, according to the cause of the neglect, which is usually just some form of laziness.

✠

CHAPTER III

✠

CONDITIONS FOR PRAYER

Before we look at specific kinds of prayers, it is a good idea to look at the general conditions of prayer. This part of our guide takes a look at the "big picture"—the general characteristics of prayer.

To Whom May We Pray?

Although God the Father is mentioned in the Lord's Prayer as the one to whom we are to pray, it is not out of place to address our prayers to the other divine persons. The special appeal to one does not exclude the others.

More commonly, the Father is addressed in the beginning of the prayers of the Church, though they close with the invocation, "Through Our Lord Jesus Christ, thy Son, who with thee liveth and reigneth in the unity of the Holy Ghost, world without end." If the prayer is addressed to God the Son, the conclusion is: "Who livest and reignest with God the Father in the unity of the Holy Ghost, God, world without end"; or, "Who with Thee liveth and reigneth in the unity of the Holy Spirit." (I have used some traditional language here to emphasize the point.)

Prayer may be addressed to Christ as man, because he is a divine person, not, however, to his human nature as such, precisely because prayer must always be addressed to a person, never to something impersonal or in the abstract. An appeal to anything impersonal, as for instance to the heart, the wounds, the cross of Christ, must be taken figuratively as intended for Christ himself.

Who Can Pray?

As Christ has promised to intercede for us (St. John 14:16) and is said to do so (Romans 8:34; Hebrews 7:25), we may ask his intercession. He prays in virtue of his own merits, and the saints intercede for us in virtue of his merits. Consequently, for those of us who pray with the saints, it is to ask for their intercession in our behalf, not to expect that they can bestow gifts on us of their own power.

The just can pray, and sinners too, or, rather, especially. No matter how hardened we may become in sin, we need and are bound to pray to be delivered from sin and from the temptations which confront us. The sinner's prayer could offend God only if it were hypocritical or presumptuous, for example, if he were to ask God to let him continue in his evil course.

Conditions of Prayer

In the first place, as we have said above, the object must be *worthy* of God and good for the one who prays, spiritually or temporally. This condition is always implied in the prayer of one who is resigned to God's will, who is ready to accept any spiritual favor God may be pleased to grant, and who wants temporal favors only insofar as they may help to serve God.

Next, you need *faith*, not only the general belief that God is capable of answering prayer or that it is a powerful means of obtaining his favor, but also *implicit trust* in God's fidelity to his promise to hear a prayer in some particular instance. This trust implies a special act of faith and hope that if our request is for our good, God will grant it, or something else equivalent or better, which in his wisdom he deems best for us.

Prayer should be *humble*. To ask as if one has a binding claim on God's goodness or warrant to obtain some favor would not be prayer but demand. The parable of the Pharisee and the publican illustrates this very clearly, and there are innumerable testimonies in scripture to the power of humility in prayer. "A contrite and humbled heart, O God, thou wilt not despise" (Psalm 1:19). "The prayer of him that humbleth himself shall pierce the clouds" (Ecclesiastes 35:21). We should try to be sure that our conscience is good and that there is no defect in our conduct inconsistent with prayer.

Sincerity is another necessary condition for prayer. It would be idle to ask favor without doing everything in our own power to obtain it, to beg for it without really wishing for it, or, at the same time that you pray, to do anything inconsistent with the prayer.

Earnestness or *fervor* is another quality of prayer. Avoid all lukewarm or halfhearted petitions. To be resigned to God's will in prayer does not imply that you should be indifferent in the sense that you do not care whether prayers are heard. On the contrary, true resignation to God's will is possible only after we have desired and earnestly expressed our desire in prayer for such things as seem needful to do his will. This earnestness is the element which makes the persevering prayer so well described in such parables as the Friend at Midnight (St. Luke 11:5–8), the Widow and the Unjust Judge (St. Luke 18:2–5), and which ultimately obtains the precious gift of perseverance in grace.

Prayer should be a *habit*. To cultivate the habit, St. Ignatius of Loyola recommends in his *Spiritual Exercises* that one should recite often certain familiar prayers, such as the Lord's Prayer, the Angelus, or the Creeds, slowly enough to admit the interval of a breath between the principal words or sentences, so you will have time to think of their meaning and to feel in your heart the appropriate emotions.

Another practice St. Ignatius strongly recommends is to take each sentence of these prayers as a subject of reflection, not delaying too long on any one of them unless one finds in it some suggestion or helpful thought or sentiment, but then stopping to reflect as long as you find proper food for thought or emotion, and, when you have dwelt sufficiently on any passage, finishing the prayer without further deliberate reflection.

Postures in Prayer

Postures in prayer are an evidence of the tendency in human nature to express inward sentiment by outward sign. Not only among Jews and Christians, but among pagan peoples also, certain postures have been considered appropriate in prayer, for instance, standing with arms raised as did the Romans.

For example, the *Orante* indicates the postures favored by the early Christians, standing with hands extended, as Christ on the cross, or with hands raised towards heaven. Typically, this is the posture in which you see priests during the Mass. Among the faithful, you will see bowed heads, kneeling, or kneeling with eyes raised toward heaven. Prostration, kneeling, genuflection, and such gestures as striking the breast are all outward signs of the reverence proper for prayer, whether in public or private.

What Is the Sign of the Cross?

Not all prayer is verbal; indeed, there are many "physical" prayers used by Christians. The sign of the Cross is a prayer which reminds us of two important mysteries of our faith: the Blessed Trinity and redemption. As we say the prayer, we trace the cross from our forehead to our chest and from one shoulder to the other. We are literally "signing" ourselves with the cross. The mysteries of the Trinity and redemption are expressed in the sign of the cross.

When we say "In the name," we express the truth that there is one God. When we say, "of the Father, and of the Son, and of the Holy Ghost [Holy Spirit]," we show our belief that there are three distinct persons in God. When we make the form of the Cross on ourselves, we express our belief that the Son of God-made-man redeemed us by his death on the Cross.

We usually make the sign of the Cross when we begin and end our prayers and when we enter and leave a church.

✠

CHAPTER IV

✟

GENERAL TYPES AND CONDITIONS

Vocal Prayer

Prayer may be vocal (spoken) or mental, private or public. In vocal prayer, some outward action, usually verbal expression, accompanies the internal act implied in every form of prayer. This external action not only helps to keep us attentive to the prayer, but it also adds to its intensity.

Examples occur in the prayer of the Israelites in captivity (Exodus 2:23), again after their idolatry among the Canaanites (Judges 3:9), the Lord's Prayer (St. Matthew 9:9), Christ's own prayer after raising Lazarus (St. John 11:41), and the testimonies in Hebrews 5:7 and 13:15. Frequently, in practices common to the Church from her beginning, we are called to use hymns, canticles, and other vocal forms of prayer.

Mental Prayer

Meditation is a form of mental prayer consisting of the application of the various faculties of the soul, memory, imagination, intellect, and will to the consideration of some mystery, principle, truth, or fact. We meditate with a view to awakening proper spiritual emotions, focusing on some act or course of action regarded as God's will, and as a means of union with him. In some degree or other, it has always been practiced by God-fearing souls.

There is abundant evidence of this in the Old Testament, as, for instance, in Psalms 38:4, 62:7, 76:13, and 118 (throughout); Ecclesiasticus 14:22; Isaiah 26:9 and 58:1; and Jeremiah 12:11. In the New Testament, Christ gave frequent examples of mental prayer, and St. Paul often refers to it, as in Ephesians 6:18, Colossians 4:2, I Timothy 4:15, and I Corinthians 14:15.

The writings of the fathers and of the great theologians are in large measure the fruit of devout meditation and study of the mysteries of religion. Particular forms of mental prayer do not seem to have had a uniform rule or practice. The monastic rules generally prescribed times for common prayer, usually the recitation of the Office, leaving it to the individual to ponder as he might on one or other of the texts.

Early in the sixteenth century, the Dominican chapter of Milan prescribed mental prayer for half an hour morning and evening. Among the Franciscans, there is record of methodical mental prayer from about the middle of that century. The Carmelites had no formal rule for mental prayer until Saint Teresa introduced it for two hours daily in the sixteenth century.

Set Prayer and Spontaneous Prayer

The concept of prayer and the many ways individuals pray could fill volumes and reveal just the tip of the iceberg on the subject. We will examine a few types of prayers and emphasize that there is no better or poorer method. Instead, you must develop your own spiritual direction, plan, or program—your own personal relationship with God. Indeed, forming a pattern of prayer is coming to understand yourself, it is part of your personal growth, and it is a thing that may change over time as you grow.

To paraphrase the words of Ecclesiastes, "There is a time and a season for everything." There are differences between rote or memorized prayer and what some call prayers from the heart, or extemporaneous prayer.

Classically, many denominations have prayers that are called rote prayer. These are memorized in a similar fashion to how we Americans memorize the Pledge of Allegiance or our national anthem. These become parts of the culture of that religious denomination and part of most worship ceremonies. In fact, the simple "Amen" is a part of most endings to prayers throughout Christian denominations.

Strengths and weaknesses are inherent in any type of prayer, and we should look at some of the strengths and weaknesses of rote prayer.

One of the criticisms that critics usually level is that, because the words are memorized and said again and again in rote fashion, in many cases, the person loses the real meaning of the words he or she is praying. We can quickly recite the memorized prayer, especially if we have repeated it many times in worship. However, we may not think about the words or have faith in what we are saying.

What becomes familiar is often not really understood or sometimes taken for granted. In this respect, rote prayer can lull someone into a sense of security without substance. They are praying what amounts to mumbo jumbo *if* they do not understand the content of what they are praying or are not mindful of what they are saying.

On the other hand, rote prayer has some very important strengths. A priest at a retreat once said that he sat down and prayed a rote prayer with an elderly patient dying in a nursing home. The patient did not really seem to connect with the world. However, when the priest began to pray that memorized prayer with her, she started to repeat the words with him. A connection had been made through the haze of her dying and her dementia, and she was able to join the clergyman in prayer.

This illustrates one of the great strengths of rote prayer; it allows us a connection when we are under stress, a quick way of accessing comfort, a path that is well traveled for our minds but still has meaning to us by the familiarity of the words and the comfort we have from previous association.

Another strength of rote prayer is that it provides people who have memorized these prayers with a sense of community, a sense of belonging. It is very comforting to enter a worship service and be familiar with the songs or prayers in that service, especially if you are visiting a church other than the one you call home. Rote or memorized prayers create community and culture, as well as the continuity of passing down information and tradition to future generations and new converts. They become part of a written and oral tradition that acts as a bridge between the past and the future.

While we can see the strengths and weaknesses of rote prayer, in many cases, it seems that being objective about prayer from the heart is more difficult. However, we will attempt to point out some of the strengths and weaknesses of prayer from the heart, or extemporaneous prayer. Many of the strengths of this form of prayer are sometimes a mirror image of the weaknesses of rote prayer.

When we pray from the heart or extemporaneously, we know the words we choose, feel the words we choose, and are mentally engaged in the prayer itself. It is not something we can say while focusing on something else, as many people might say rote prayer and be thinking of what they will be doing after church or their grocery list.

When we pray off the top of our heads or from the heart, we have to think about the words, and there is usually more emotion and connection with the content involved—more involvement, more faith, perhaps, and more focus.

Another evident strength of prayer from the heart is that you can tailor it to the situation. You can craft with your words what is most appropriate for blessings or petitions without having to try to find one that has been memorized but doesn't quite fit the situation.

You also can tailor the length of the prayer, as well as content, to meet the needs of the situation. Beyond the situation you are in, prayer from the heart may more completely fit the emotions you are feeling than a memorized prayer. This form of prayer can be far more flexible than rote prayer.

However, extemporaneous prayer can have its disadvantages. When we are under pressure or stress—let's face it—sometimes we go blank. It is at times like these that prayer from the heart is sometimes difficult and having memorized prayer or rote prayers to fall back on can be important.

In many cases, we seem to infuse our prayer with whatever emotions we are feeling. When we are depressed, we want to feel comfort and not more depression. Rote prayers can bring that sense of comfort based on past memories associated with those prayers, that sense of community praying with you the same prayer.

Whatever means of prayer you might choose, looking at these two forms can help you understand that there are many paths and means of communication and some of the strengths and weaknesses of each. Perhaps, there is a time and season for many types of prayers depending on where you are in your life. Indeed, you might have many types of prayer in your life depending on the circumstances.

✠

Chapter V

What Types of Prayer Are There?

Now that we have looked at what prayer is and why we should pray, we have come to the part of our *field guide* on how to identify types of prayer. It is a bit like spotting birds or identifying plants, except without the bug bites and the sunburn!

There are a number of prayer types, and most can truly be found at all times and in all places.

Blessing and Adoration

We *bless* God because he is the source of every blessing. Let's look at a couple of examples:

Psalm 24:9–10

> 9: Lift up your heads, O gates! and be lifted up, O ancient doors! that the King of glory may come in.
>
> 10: Who is this King of glory? The LORD of hosts, he is the King of glory! [Selah]

Psalm 95:1–6

> 1: O come, let us sing to the LORD; let us make a joyful noise to the rock of our salvation!
>
> 2: Let us come into his presence with thanksgiving; let us make a joyful noise to him with songs of praise!
>
> 3: For the LORD is a great God, and a great King above all gods.
>
> 4: In his hand are the depths of the earth; the heights of the mountains are his also.
>
> 5: The sea is his, for he made it; for his hands formed the dry land.
>
> 6: O come, let us worship and bow down, let us kneel before the LORD, our Maker!

II Corinthians 1:3–7

> 3: Blessed be the God and Father of our Lord Jesus Christ, the Father of mercies and God of all comfort,
>
> 4: who comforts us in all our affliction, so that we may be able to comfort those who are in any affliction, with the comfort with which we ourselves are comforted by God.
>
> 5: For as we share abundantly in Christ's sufferings, so through Christ we share abundantly in comfort too.
>
> 6: If we are afflicted, it is for your comfort and salvation; and if we are comforted, it is for your comfort, which you experience when you patiently endure the same sufferings that we suffer.
>
> 7: Our hope for you is unshaken; for we know that as you share in our sufferings, you will also share in our comfort.

Adoration is a special type of prayer that involves a deep love and an awareness of God's "otherness" and our dependence on him. Two fundamental forms express this movement: Our prayer ascends in the Holy Spirit through Christ to the Father—we bless him for having blessed us; it implores the grace of the Holy Spirit that descends through Christ from the Father—he blesses us.

Adoration is the first attitude of man acknowledging that he is a creature before his creator. It exalts the greatness of the Lord who made us and the almighty power of the Savior who sets us free from evil. Adoration is homage of the spirit to the "King of Glory," respectful silence in the presence of the "ever greater" God. Adoration of the holy and sovereign God of love blends with humility and gives assurance to our supplications. Often in this form of prayer, no words are spoken. It is an attitude, a stance, taken before God's majesty. *Blessing* expresses the basic movement of Christian prayer: It is an encounter between God and man. In blessing, God's gift and man's acceptance of it are united in dialogue with each other. The prayer of blessing is man's response to God's gifts: Because God blesses, the human heart can in return bless the one who is the source of every blessing.

Petition

All our needs, including our need of forgiveness and salvation, can be included in prayers of petition, which are the most common form of prayer. We ask God for the things we need in our life, the things we need to survive: our daily bread, a roof over our heads, employment, and so on. We should not be ashamed to ask God for what we need, but we always should be attentive to the needs of others and especially to those who have little in life.

Petitions are usually self-oriented, presenting our personal needs to our Heavenly Father, in trust that he will provide. The vocabulary of supplication in the New Testament is rich in shades of meaning: ask, beseech, plead, invoke, entreat, cry out, even "struggle in prayer."

Let's have a quick look at some forms of petition.

ROMANS 8:22–28

22: We know that the whole creation has been groaning in travail together until now;

23: and not only the creation, but we ourselves, who have the first fruits of the Spirit, groan inwardly as we wait for adoption as sons, the redemption of our bodies.

24: For in this hope we were saved. Now hope that is seen is not hope. For who hopes for what he sees?

25: But if we hope for what we do not see, we wait for it with patience.

26: Likewise the Spirit helps us in our weakness; for we do not know how to pray as we ought, but the Spirit himself intercedes for us with sighs too deep for words.

27: And he who searches the hearts of men knows what is the mind of the Spirit, because the Spirit intercedes for the saints according to the will of God.

28: We know that in everything God works for good with those who love him, who are called according to his purpose.

St. Luke 18:13

But the tax collector, standing far off, would not even lift up his eyes to heaven, but beat his breast, saying, "God, be merciful to me a sinner!"

See if you can identify some of the characteristics of good prayer. Is this how we are offering our own petitions?

Petition is probably the most spontaneous form of prayer by its nature. By prayer of petition, we express awareness of our relationship with God. We are creatures who are not our own beginning, not the masters of adversity, not our own end. We are sinners who as Christians know that we have turned away from our Father, and our petition is already a turning back to him.

The first movement of the prayer of petition is asking forgiveness, like the tax collector in the parable: "God, be merciful to me a sinner!" It is a prerequisite for righteous and pure prayer. A trusting humility brings us back into the light of communion between the Father and his Son, Jesus Christ, and with one another, so that "we receive from him whatever we ask." Asking forgiveness is the requirement for both the Eucharistic liturgy and personal prayer.

Christian petition is centered on the desire and search for the kingdom to come, in keeping with the teaching of Christ. There is an order, a hierarchy, in these petitions. We pray first for the kingdom, then for what is necessary to welcome it and cooperate with its coming.

This collaboration with the mission of Christ and the Holy Spirit, which is now that of the Church, is the object of the prayer of the apostolic community. It is the prayer of St. Paul which reveals to us how his care for all the churches ought to inspire Christian prayer.

When we share in God's saving love, we understand that every need can become the object of petition. Christ, who assumed all things in order to redeem all things, is glorified by what we ask the Father in his name. It is with this confidence that St. James and St. Paul exhort us to pray constantly.

Intercession

This prayer involves asking on behalf of others. Let's have a look at some foundations of intercessory prayer.

ROMANS 8:34

[W]ho is to condemn? Is it Christ Jesus, who died, yes, who was raised from the dead, who is at the right hand of God, who indeed *intercedes* for us?

I TIMOTHY 2:5–8

5: For there is one God, and there is one mediator between God and men, the man Christ Jesus,

6: who gave himself as a ransom for all, the testimony to which was borne at the proper time.

7: For this I was appointed a preacher and apostle (I am telling the truth, I am not lying), a teacher of the Gentiles in faith and truth.

8: I desire then that in every place the men should pray, lifting holy hands without anger or quarreling …

HEBREWS 7:25

Consequently he is able for all time to save those who draw near to God through him, since he always lives to make *intercession* for them.

ACTS 12:5

So Peter was kept in prison; but earnest *prayer for him* was made to God by the Church.

Intercession is love on its knees in prayer for others. Here, we are standing in the gap, that is, praying prayers of repentance, identifying ourselves with the sins of those for whom we are in prayer. Intercession is a prayer of petition which leads us to pray as Jesus did. He is the one intercessor with the Father on behalf of all men, especially sinners. He is "able for all time to save those who draw near to God through him, since he always lives to make intercession for them" (Hebrews 7:25). The Holy Spirit "himself intercedes for us ... and intercedes for the saints according to the will of God" (Romans 8:27).

Since Abraham, intercession—asking on behalf of another—has been characteristic of a heart attuned to God's mercy. In the Church, intercession is an expression of the communion of saints. In intercession, he who prays looks "not only to his own interests, but also to the interests of others," even to the point of praying for those who do him harm.

The first Christian communities lived this form of fellowship intensely. Thus, the apostle Paul gives them a share in his ministry of preaching the Gospel but also intercedes for them. The intercession of Christians recognizes no boundaries: "for all men, for kings and all who are in high positions," for persecutors, for the salvation of those who reject the Gospel.

Here are some examples you can use:

THE INTERCESSION (1928 BOOK OF COMMON PRAYER)

AND accept, O Lord, our intercessions for all mankind. Let the light of thy Gospel shine upon all nations; and may as many as have received it, live as becomes it. Be gracious unto thy Church; and grant that every member of the same, in his vocation and ministry, may serve thee faithfully. Bless all in authority over us; and so rule their hearts and strengthen their hands, that they may punish wickedness and vice, and maintain thy true religion and virtue. Send down thy blessings, temporal and spiritual, upon all our relations, friends, and neighbours. Reward all who have done us good, and pardon all those who have done or wish us evil, and give them repentance and better minds. Be merciful to all who are in any trouble; and do thou, the

God of pity, administer to them according to their several necessities; for his sake who went about doing good, thy Son our Saviour Jesus Christ. *Amen.*

For a Sick Person (1928 Book of Common Prayer)

O Father of mercies and God of all comfort, our only help in time of need; We humbly beseech thee to behold, visit, and relieve thy sick servant [N.] for whom our prayers are desired. Look upon him with the eyes of thy mercy; comfort him with a sense of thy goodness; preserve him from the temptations of the enemy; and give him patience under his affliction. In thy good time, restore him to health, and enable him to lead the residue of his life in thy fear, and to thy glory; and grant that finally he may dwell with thee in life everlasting; through Jesus Christ our Lord. *Amen.*

Watch, O Lord (St. Augustine)

Watch, O Lord, with those who wake, or watch, or weep tonight, and give Your angels and saints charge over those who sleep.

Tend Your sick ones, O Lord Christ.

Rest Your weary ones.

Bless Your dying ones.

Soothe Your suffering ones.

Pity Your afflicted ones.

Shield Your joyous ones, and all for Your love's sake. *Amen.*

Thanksgiving

All circumstances, including joy and suffering, are reasons to give thanks. Thanksgiving is probably the highest form of prayer, often forgotten in the flurry of our petitions and yet commanded by scripture.

I THESSALONIANS 5:18

[G]ive thanks in all circumstances; for this is the will of God in Christ Jesus for you.

COLOSSIANS 4:2

Continue steadfastly in prayer, being watchful in it with *thanksgiving* ...

A grateful heart simply wants to say thanks—for life, for faith, for redemption, for others, for all things in your life. We are commanded to give thanks in all circumstances. Being thankful is being grateful for God's protection, provision, blessing, and most of all for his Son.

Thanksgiving characterizes the prayer of the Church which, in celebrating the Eucharist, reveals and becomes more fully what she is. In the work of salvation, Christ sets creation free from sin and death to consecrate it anew and make it return to the Father, for his glory. The thanksgiving of the members of the body participates in that of great thanksgiving of Christ as head of the body.

As in the prayer of petition, every event and need can become an offering of thanksgiving. The letters of St. Paul often begin and end with thanksgiving, and the Lord Jesus is always present in it: "Give thanks in all circumstances; for this is the will of God in Christ Jesus for you ..." (1 Thessalonians 5:18). "Continue steadfastly in prayer, being watchful in it with thanksgiving" (Colossians 4:1).

THE THANKSGIVING (1928 BOOK OF COMMON PRAYER)

TO our prayers, O Lord, we join our unfeigned thanks for all thy mercies; for our being, our reason, and all other endowments and faculties of soul and body; for our health, friends, food, and raiment, and all the other comforts and conveniences of life. Above all, we adore thy mercy in sending thy only Son into the world, to redeem us from sin and eternal death, and in giving us the knowledge and sense of our duty towards thee. We bless thee for thy patience with us, notwithstanding our many and great provocations; for all the directions, assistances, and comforts of thy Holy Spirit; for thy continual care and watchful providence over us through the whole course of our lives; and particularly for the mercies and benefits of the past day; beseeching thee to continue these thy blessings to us, and to give us grace to show our thankfulness in a sincere obedience to his laws, through whose merits and intercession we received them all, thy Son our Saviour Jesus Christ. *Amen.*

Praise

Praise is the form of prayer which recognizes most immediately that God is God. It lauds God for his own sake and gives him glory, quite beyond what he does, but simply because *he is*. It shares in the blessed happiness of the pure of heart who love God in faith before seeing him in glory. Once again, let's turn to the Bible:

ROMANS 8:16

[I]t is the Spirit himself bearing witness with our spirit that we are children of God ...

ACTS 2:46–47

And day by day, attending the temple together and breaking bread in their homes, they partook of food with glad and generous hearts, *praising* God and having favor with all the people. And the Lord added to their number day by day those who were being saved.

ACTS 4:21

And when they had further threatened them, they let them go, finding no way to punish them, because of the people; for all men *praised* God for what had happened.

PSALM 92

A Psalm. A Song for the Sabbath.

1: It is good to give thanks to the LORD, to sing praises to thy name, O Most High;

2: to declare thy steadfast love in the morning, and thy faithfulness by night,

3: to the music of the lute and the harp, to the melody of the lyre.

4: For thou, O LORD, hast made me glad by thy work; at the works of thy hands I sing for joy.

5: How great are thy works, O LORD! Thy thoughts are very deep!

6: The dull man cannot know, the stupid cannot understand this:

7: that, though the wicked sprout like grass and all evildoers flourish, they are doomed to destruction for ever,

8: but thou, O LORD, art on high for ever.

9: For, lo, thy enemies, O LORD, for, lo, thy enemies shall perish; all evildoers shall be scattered.

10: But thou hast exalted my horn like that of the wild ox; thou hast poured over me fresh oil.

11: My eyes have seen the downfall of my enemies, my ears have heard the doom of my evil assailants.

12: The righteous flourish like the palm tree, and grow like a cedar in Lebanon.

13: They are planted in the house of the LORD, they flourish in the courts of our God.

14: They still bring forth fruit in old age, they are ever full of sap and green,

15: to show that the LORD is upright; he is my rock, and there is no unrighteousness in him.

By praise, the Spirit is joined to our spirits to bear witness that we are children of God, testifying to the only Son in whom we are adopted and by whom we glorify the Father. Praise embraces the other forms of prayer and carries them toward him who is its source and goal: the "one God, the Father, from whom are all things and for whom we exist."

"[Address] one another in psalms and hymns and spiritual songs, singing and making melody to the Lord with all your heart." Like the inspired writers of the New Testament, the first Christian communities read the book of Psalms in a new way, singing in it the mystery of Christ.

In the newness of the Spirit, they also composed hymns and canticles in the light of the unheard-of event that God accomplished in his Son: his incarnation, his death which conquered death, and his resurrection and ascension to the right hand of the Father. doxology, the praise of God, arises from this "marvelous work" of the whole economy of salvation.

The Eucharist contains and expresses all forms of prayer: It is "the pure offering" of the whole body of Christ to the glory of God's name, and according to the traditions of East and West, it is the "sacrifice of praise."

✝

CHAPTER VI

PLACES FOR PRAYER

"IT is very meet, right, and our bounden duty, that we should at all times, and in all places, give thanks unto thee, O Lord, Holy Father, Almighty, Everlasting God."

—*The 1928 Book of Common Prayer*

Prayer at Home

Prayer in the home is an essential. To start your day with morning or evening prayer from the prayer books—in the examples below the Anglican 1928 Book of Common Prayer—is a great thing, particularly if your whole family joins in. However, with schedules for school and work, families on the move, and the problems of getting everyone in the same place twice a day, this is often just not practical. But you can make your home a center of prayer by doing these prayers yourself.

No time, you say? Well, there are prayers that can start and end the day—short, but powerful prayers, that begin and end the day in Christ. Here are some examples:

MORNING *(1928 BOOK OF COMMON PRAYER, PAGE 594)*

O GOD, the King eternal, who dividest the day from the darkness, and turnest the shadow of death into the morning; Drive far off from us all wrong desires, incline our hearts to keep thy law, and guide our feet into the way of peace; that having done thy will with cheerfulness while it was day, we may, when the night cometh, rejoice to give thee thanks; through Jesus Christ our Lord. *Amen.*

NIGHT *(1928 BOOK OF COMMON PRAYER, PAGE 594)*

O LORD, support us all the day long, until the shadows lengthen and the evening comes, and the busy world is hushed, and the fever of life is over, and our work is done. Then in thy mercy grant us a safe lodging, and a holy rest, and peace at the last. *Amen.*

Take a moment and say these prayers. Pretty fast, eh? Now try saying each of them without a distracting thought creeping in. Not so fast!

If you have small children in your family, you can teach them the Lord's Prayer. Encourage them to say it when you say your morning and evening prayers.

Finally, always remember a prayer of thanksgiving at mealtime (whether at home or on the road). This is one for the family to say as often as you can share a meal in one place at the same time.

GRACE BEFORE MEAL

BLESS, O Father, thy gifts to our use and us to thy service; for Christ's sake. *Amen.*

Or

GIVE us grateful hearts, our Father, for all thy mercies, and make us mindful of the needs of others; through Jesus Christ our Lord. *Amen.*

Prayer on the Road

Now that society values its "road warriors," we spend ever-increasing amounts of time just getting places. So, it is time to take a moment to focus on "road prayers." You could, and should, pray throughout your day when you are not otherwise occupied. This is called, "Praying into the interstices (small openings of time) of the day."

This prayer doesn't have to be obvious—folks do tend to stare at those doing vocal prayer on the subway. However, your mental prayers can be offered to God anywhere, at any time. In fact, finger rosaries and short prayer ropes can be used for the silent prayer of the rosary or the Jesus Prayer. In fact, you can even pray silently the prayers of the Book of Common Prayer!

Caught in traffic? Pray the rosary or recite the Jesus Prayer. It is far better for you than that cellular telephone call you would make and far less dangerous.

The key is to turn your prayer life into a prayer attitude, an attitude of praise and thanksgiving for the gifts of God that operate all of the time. Simple tasks, even unpleasant or repetitious works, can be dedicated to the glory of God in prayer.

One intercessory prayer technique that I use (although not often enough!) is to pray during exercise, such as running or cycling. You can offer each mile for a specific intercession or thanksgiving. Not only are you praying in an otherwise downtime, but you will be surprised at how fast those miles go by.

A Special Note on Prayer Walking

Recent years have seen a surge of intercessors walking through their neighborhoods, praying both silently and aloud for their neighbors. Other intercessors have followed the leading of the Holy Spirit to travel to distant lands to intercede for the lost peoples of those places.

A study of the early chapters of Genesis reveals that in the beginning, man and woman were created to walk with God. Men such as Enoch and Noah are described as ones who "walked with God."

It is God's intention that we experience this most intimate and confidential of relationships with him. Rebellion brought an end to the "walk," but God through Christ redeemed us that we might again walk with him.

Now in the twenty-first century, as world evangelism accelerates, the people of God are doing a "new" thing. Beginning in the mid-1970s, believers throughout the world again began to sense his leading us to move out of our church buildings to intercede in the world. This kind of moving, on-site intercession has become known as prayer walking. It is walking and talking with God, hearing and heeding his voice, seeing and sensing as he does. In many ways, this is reminiscent of the monks who wandered Medieval Europe to offer prayers in troubled times. Now, in a darkening and difficult world, many of the faithful are called to follow this pattern.

For a number of reasons, much of Christ's Church has become distanced from God and from the world to which she is called. Prayer walking has shown itself to be a divine solution to both of these problems. As God leads us into a closer walk with him, we simultaneously find ourselves in closer proximity to our lost world.

Walking with him, we see as he sees and respond with pointed, empowered intercession. Then as he answers these insightful, on-site prayers, we are right where we need to be to extend a touch of love and share a word of hope. Truly, the prayer-walking Church brings great good to its neighborhood and its world.

Types of Prayer Walking

DEVOTIONAL
All prayer walking begins with and then issues from our personal prayer walk with God. Ensure that the most important goal in your life is nurturing a pure and unhindered walk with God.

INCIDENTAL
As we walk with God through the responsibilities and activities of our day, we will find Christ prompting us to intercede for others around us. This is incidental prayer walking—incidental to our normal work in the world. God uses us as intercessors.

INTENTIONAL
Strategically important are our planned and organized times of on-site intercession as God directs. These could be as simple as an evening prayer walk through our neighborhood or as involved as leading a prayer team overseas. Planned, intentional prayer walks are powerful for preparing the way for witness and ministry in Jesus's name.

The talking Church sounds good. The walking Church looks good. The prayer-walking Church brings good.

Prayer in Church

In the Church, there is a refuge from the vanity and the storms of life. Here is the calm harbor for souls seeking after salvation. Here is incorruptible food and drink for the soul. Here is the light that enlightens all men existing upon earth. Here is the clean air of the spirit. Here is the fountain of living water which flows to life eternal (St. John 4:14). Here are distributed the gifts of the Holy Spirit. Here is the cleansing of souls.

The reading and chanting that is done in the Church is done in a holy language. All Christians should learn it, so they can better understand the wonderful teachings of the Church, who educates her children to prepare them for heaven, for life eternal.

In the house of God, we comprehend the truly noble origin of our souls, the worth of life and its goal and purpose. We are torn away from our fascination with earthly things, the toys and the noise and the passions of the day. In the house of God, we comprehend our temporal and eternal fate. Here the Savior lives—in his life-giving mysteries, in his salvation. Here we recognize our true relationship to God and to our neighbor, to our family and to the society in which we live.

Our churches are a bit of heaven on earth, a place where intimate union with the divine takes place. It is a heavenly school, where Christians are taught to become citizens of heaven, where they are taught heavenly norms and the way of life in heaven. It is the threshold of heaven, a place of communal prayer, thanksgiving, and praise of the Triune God, creator and protector of all. It is a place of unification with the angels.

What is more honorable and more esteemed than the temple? Nothing. In its divine services, as in a blueprint, are severally depicted the fates of all humanity, from beginning to end. The divine services are the alpha and omega of the world and of mankind (*from Holy Righteous St. John of Kronstadt*).

Prayer Groups

Here is another world-changing aspect of prayer life. You can organize your own prayer group or circle. You can physically meet, usually at a home, to share scripture and to pray. Here is an outline for organizing a prayer group that works for campus-, home-, and work-based groups as well.

PRAY. Be sure that this is the direction God wants you to go. Remember Proverbs 3:5–6: "Trust in the Lord with all your heart and lean not on your own understanding; in all your ways acknowledge Him, and He will direct your paths."

BE ORGANIZED. Write out a charter that describes the purpose of your club or group. This is useful even if you are forming a home- or work-based group so that you can tell others what your group is about. Find a convenient time for people to meet. Plan how long you want meetings to be and how the meetings should be arranged.

FIND A SPONSOR. Most schools will require you to have a faculty sponsor. You and a friend should choose a candidate then politely ask that person if he or she would be willing to be your sponsor.

FIND PEOPLE TO HELP YOU. It's impossible to do all the work by yourself to make your group successful; not only that, it's not what God wants you to do! "Two are better than one, because they have a good reward for their labor" (Ecclesiastes 4:9; also see Exodus 18:13–26). Find some people who can help and divide up the tasks.

BE SURE EVERYTHING IS READY. Have all materials (devotionals, extra Bibles, prayer cards, etc.) ready beforehand. Make sure to reserve the room you are meeting in if you are not a home-based group. Be early to the meeting and have everything set up before people arrive.

How Can I Promote My Prayer Group?

ASK THE ADMINISTRATION. Once you have a sponsor for a school-based group, set a meeting with your school administrator (or whoever is in charge of clubs or groups) and present your request and your charter.

MAKE POSTERS. Put posters on bulletin boards, lockers, in the cafeteria, in bathrooms, and on school entrances where everyone will see them. Be creative in your placement, but be sure that you have permission from the appropriate body—the administration, student government, or similar group—before you start posting.

INVOLVE LOCAL MINISTERS. Ask local pastors to pray for you and mention when and where your group is meeting during their youth groups. Try to get several youth groups involved.

EXTEND PERSONAL INVITATIONS. This is often the most effective method. Have each person in your group invite two or three people.

USE THE PUBLIC ADDRESS SYSTEM. See if your principal will allow you to promote your club during regular announcements.

A QUICK REMINDER: If school officials exclude your group from facilities or services that other groups are allowed to use, they may be violating your rights. For more information, get in touch with the Alliance Defense Fund through their Web site: http://www.alliancedefensefund. org/ Do not be angry or contentious, but "Let all things be done decently and in order" (I Corinthians 14:40).

These are experienced people who can help you overcome hostility to prayer. One other thing: Be sure to pray for those who persecute you.

✠

CHAPTER VII

✠

SOME PRAYERS TO USE

There are many, many sources of prayers that you can access. The number of prayer books and devotional guides seems to grow by the day. There are some suggestions for you in this chapter and in the Suggested Reading section of this field guide, as well as some of my favorites for you to use.

Prayers in the 1928 Book of Common Prayer

Regardless of your denomination or faith community, the Book of Common Prayer has many great and powerful prayers you can use for different circumstances and events in your life.

There are prayers for healing, graces for meals, birthday prayers, and prayers of thanksgiving. There are even prayers for the weather. Here are a couple of great prayers by way of example:

FOR THE SPIRIT OF PRAYER

ALMIGHTY God, who pourest out on all who desire it, the spirit of grace and of supplication; Deliver us, when we draw nigh to thee, from coldness of heart and wanderings of mind, that with stedfast thoughts and kindled affections, we may worship thee in spirit and in truth; through Jesus Christ our Lord. *Amen.*

As we have seen, the advantage to the prayers you find in devotionals, the Book of Common Prayer or the Liturgy of the Hours are that you don't have to struggle to find the right words—they are there for you. These are prayers worked out by other faithful Christians for our use over many years. We can build on and get great help from their prayer lives by using these prayers in our devotions each day.

The Jesus Prayer

Many of the ancient and modern mystics have spoken and written about the "Jesus Prayer," citing it as one of the simplest but most powerful elements of their spirituality. It remains very popular among people today as a meditative prayer practice.

The words of this ancient prayer are *"Lord Jesus Christ, Son of God, have mercy on me, a sinner."* Some people leave out the words "a sinner," and others prefer to use the plural form, "us." Many people repeat the sentence silently for fifteen to twenty minutes each day at a specific time they set aside for contemplative prayer. Others simply pray it throughout the day as time permits, such as on their lunch break, during a commute, or while they exercise.

Bishop Diadochus, who lived in the 400s, was among the first spiritual writers to write about a repeated remembrance of Jesus's name, though the full prayer itself is first found in a sixth-century book called *The Life of Abba Philemon.* Diadochus taught that repeated prayer leads to inner stillness.

The Jesus Prayer is also called the Prayer of the Heart. One author writes, "There is within us a space, a field of the heart, in which we find a Divine Reality, and from which we are called to live. The mind, then, is to descend into that inner sanctuary, by means of the Jesus Prayer or wordless contemplation, and to stay there throughout our active day, and evening. We descend with our mind into our heart, and we live there."

Prayers from Devotionals and Guides

There are many prayers you can use from various devotionals and guides. One of the best is *St. Augustine's Prayer Book*, which is full of prayers for all occasions, including the Angelus, rosaries, and prayers relating to the Holy Eucharist. These should not be considered as substitutes for the Book of Common Prayer or the Liturgy of the Hours, but as complementary to them.

Here's an example from an online devotional:

A MORNING PRAYER WRITTEN BY ST. THERESE

> O my God! I offer Thee all my actions of this day for the intentions and for the glory of the Sacred Heart of Jesus. I desire to sanctify every beat of my heart, my every thought, my simplest works, by uniting them to Its infinite merits; and I wish to make reparation for my sins by casting them into the furnace of Its Merciful Love.

> O my God! I ask of Thee for myself and for those whom I hold dear, the grace to fulfill perfectly Thy Holy Will, to accept for love of Thee the joys and sorrows of this passing life, so that we may one day be united together in heaven for all Eternity.

> *Amen.*

Psalms

Among the wonderful prayers in the Bible, the book of Psalms—which is found in the Old Testament—stands out. There are one hundred and fifty psalms, magnificent prayers and hymns for every religious desire and need, mood, and feeling. In poetic form, the Psalms express religious experience that is valid for all ages and places. The following are suggested psalms to pray for special needs.

- When tired or upset:
  Psalm 4

- When discouraged:
  Psalm 42
- When alone or disillusioned by a friend:
  Psalm 40
- When filled with great happiness:
  Psalms 97 and **99**
- When grateful for the gifts of God:
  Psalm 135
- When in need of refuge:
  Psalm 46
- When life needs a spiritual boost:
  Psalm 27
- When worried:
  Psalm 34
- When anguished in life:
  Psalms 31 and **34**
- When in need of confidence and courage:
  Psalms 27, 31, 56, and **62**
- When in need of health:
  Psalms 6, 27, 39, and **41**

The Rosary

ORIGINS

Fr. William Saunders, former president of then Notre Dame Institute (now the Notre Dame Institute of Christendom College), in a short article, tells us that the origins of the rosary are "sketchy" at best. The use of prayer beads and the repeated recitation of prayers to aid in meditation stem from the earliest days of the Church and are rooted in pre-Christian times. Evidence exists from the Middle Ages that strings of beads were used to count Our Fathers and Hail Marys.

The structure of the rosary gradually evolved between the twelfth and fifteenth centuries. Eventually, fifty Hail Marys were recited and linked with verses of psalms or other phrases evoking the lives of Jesus and Mary. At this time, this prayer form became known as the rosarium ("rose garden"), actually a common term to designate a collection of similar materials, such as an anthology of stories on the same subject or theme. During the sixteenth century, the structure of the five-decade rosary based on the three sets of mysteries prevailed.

Tradition holds that St. Dominic (d. 1221) devised the rosary as we know it. Moved by a vision of the Virgin Mary, he preached the use of the rosary in his missionary work among the Albigensians, heretics who had denied the mystery of Christ. Some scholars take exception to St. Dominic's role in forming the rosary. The earliest accounts of his life do not mention it, the Dominican constitutions do not link him with it, and some contemporaneous portraits do not include it as a symbol to identify the saint.

In 1922, Dom Louis Cougaud stated, "The various elements which enter into the composition of that Catholic devotion commonly called the rosary are the product of a long and gradual development which began before St. Dominic's time, which continued without his having any share in it, and which only attained its final shape several centuries after his death." However, others believe that St. Dominic not so much "invented" the rosary as he preached its use to convert sinners and those who had strayed from the faith.

The rosary gained greater popularity in the 1500s, when the Moslem Turks were ravaging Eastern Europe. Recall that in 1453, Constantinople had fallen to the Moslems, leaving the Balkans and Hungary open to conquest. With Moslems raiding even the coast of Italy, the control of the Mediterranean was at stake.

In 1571, Pope Pius V organized a fleet under the command of Don Juan of Austria, the half-brother of King Philip II of Spain. While preparations were underway, the pope asked all of the faithful to say the rosary and implore the Virgin Mary's prayers, under the title Our Lady of Victory, that our Lord would grant victory to the Christians. Although the Moslem fleet outnumbered that of the Christians in both vessels and sailors, the forces were ready to meet in battle. The Christian flagship flew a blue banner depicting Christ crucified. On October 7, 1571, the Moslems were defeated at the Battle of Lepanto. The following year, Pope St. Pius V established the Feast of the Holy Rosary on October 7, where the faithful would not only remember this victory, but also give thanks to the Lord for all of his benefits and remember the powerful intercession of the Blessed Virgin.

The prayers of the rosary, reflecting on the life of Christ, are used not only by Catholic Christians of all kinds, but increasingly in other Christian faith communities.

HOW TO PRAY THE ROSARY

1. While holding the crucifix, make the sign of the Cross and then recite the Apostles' Creed.

2. Recite the Our Father on the first large (or single) bead.

3. On each of the three small beads, recite a Hail Mary for an increase of faith, hope, and charity.

4. Recite the Glory Be to the Father after the third Hail Mary.

5. Recall the first Rosary Mystery and then recite the Our Father on the next large bead.

6. On each of the adjacent ten small beads (also referred to as a decade) recite a Hail Mary while reflecting on the first mystery.

7. After the tenth Hail Mary, recite a Glory Be to the Father.

8. Each succeeding decade is prayed in a similar manner by recalling the appropriate mystery and reciting an Our Father, ten Hail Marys, and the Glory Be to the Father, while reflecting on the mystery.

9. When the fifth mystery is completed, the rosary is customarily concluded with a Hail Holy Queen, and then the closing prayer(s).

10. For the intentions of the welfare of the Church on Earth, one may recite at the end of the rosary one Our Father, one Hail Mary, and one Glory Be.

The Five Joyful Mysteries

The Annunciation of Our Lord
(Luke 1:26–33, 38)

The angel Gabriel was sent from God to a town of Galilee named Nazareth, to a virgin betrothed to a man named Joseph, of the house of David. The virgin's name was Mary. Upon arriving, the angel said to her, "Rejoice, O highly favored daughter! The Lord is with you. Blessed are you among women." She was deeply troubled by his words, and wondered what his greeting meant. The angel went on to say to her: "Do not fear, Mary. You have found favor with God. You shall conceive and bear a son and give him the name Jesus. Great will be his dignity and he will be called Son of the Most High. The Lord God will give him the throne of David his father. He will rule over the house of Jacob forever and his reign will be without end."

Mary said, "I am the servant of the Lord. Let it be done to me as you say." With that, the angel left her.

Meditation: Consider the initial fear of Mary at the approach of the angel, but as soon as she was certain that her visitor was from heaven, she opened her heart to the plan laid before her, submitting herself entirely to what was being asked of her. Am I as prudent and as open to God's will as Mary?

- *Our Father, Ten Hail Marys, Glory Be*

The Visitation
(Luke 1:39–45)

Mary set out, proceeding in haste into the hill country to a town of Judah, where she entered Zechariah's house and greeted Elizabeth. When Elizabeth heard Mary's greeting, the baby leapt in her womb. Elizabeth was filled with the Holy Spirit and cried out in a loud voice: "Blest are you among women and blest is the fruit of your womb. But who am I that the mother of my Lord should come to me? The moment your greeting sounded in my ears, the baby leapt in my womb for joy. Blest is she who trusted that the Lord's words to her would be fulfilled."

Meditation: Consider how Mary thought nothing of herself in this mystery; her needs were secondary to those of her cousin, to whom she went 'with great haste.' Am I as charitable toward others? Does my own charity ask for something in return, or is it as truly selfless and immediate as that displayed by the mother of God?

- *OUR FATHER, TEN HAIL MARYS, GLORY BE....*

THE THIRD JOYFUL MYSTERY

The Nativity of Jesus
(Luke 2:6–12)

While they were in Bethlehem, the days of her confinement were completed. She gave birth to her first-born son and wrapped him in swaddling clothes and laid him in a manger, because there was no room for them in the place where travelers lodged. There were shepherds in that region living in the fields and keeping night watch by turns over their flock. The angel of the Lord appeared to them, and the glory of the Lord shone around them, and they were very much afraid. The angel said to them: "You have nothing to fear! I come to proclaim good news to you tidings of great joy to be shared by the whole people. This day in David's city a savior has been born to you, the Messiah and Lord. Let this be a sign to you: In a manger you will find an infant wrapped in swaddling clothes."

Meditation: Consider how the Holy Family were truly poor, having not even a place to stay where Mary could give birth to her son, and yet despite this, Mary and Joseph remained entirely serene and joyful. Does my happiness depend on material satisfaction, or do I possess the true joy and serenity of Mary?

- *OUR FATHER, TEN HAIL MARYS, GLORY BE ...*

THE FOURTH JOYFUL MYSTERY

The Presentation in the Temple
(Luke 2:25–32)

There lived in Jerusalem at the time a certain man named Simeon. He was just and pious, and awaited consolation of Israel, and the Holy Spirit was upon him. It was revealed to him by the Holy Spirit that he would not experience death until he had seen the Anointed of the Lord. He came to the temple now, inspired by the Spirit; and when the parents brought in the child Jesus to perform for him the customary ritual of the law, he took him in his arms and blessed God in these words: "Now, Master, you can dismiss your servant in peace; you have fulfilled your word. For my eyes have witnessed your saving deed displayed for all the peoples to see: A revealing light to the Gentiles, the glory of your people Israel."

Meditation: Consider the purity and perpetual virginity of Mary. Am I attached to worldly pleasures or is my own heart as truly pure and centered on God as is the Blessed Virgin Mary?

- *OUR FATHER, TEN HAIL MARYS, GLORY BE …*

THE FIFTH JOYFUL MYSTERY

The Finding in the Temple
(Luke 2:41–50)

The parents of Jesus used to go every year to Jerusalem for the feast of the Passover, and when he was twelve they went up for the celebration as was their custom. As they were returning at the end of the feast, the child Jesus remained behind unknown to his parents. Thinking he was in the party, they continued on their journey for a day, looking for him among their relatives and acquaintances. Not finding him, they returned to Jerusalem in search of him. On the third day, they came upon him in the temple sitting in the midst of the teachers, listening to them and asking them questions. All who heard him were amazed at his intelligence and his answers. When his parents saw him they were astonished, and his mother said to him: "Son, why have you done this to us? You see that your father and I have been searching for you in sorrow."

He said to them: "Why did you search for me? Did you not know I had to be in my Father's house?" But they did not grasp what he said to them.

Meditation: Consider how Mary sought God every day of her earthly life, in the mundane activities as well as in the great events related in scripture; do I complain about my earthly duties and responsibilities, or do I use them as opportunities to seek and to find God, following Mary's example?

- *OUR FATHER, TEN HAIL MARYS, GLORY BE ...*

The Five Sorrowful Mysteries

THE FIRST SORROWFUL MYSTERY

The Agony in the Garden
(Luke 22:39–46)

Jesus went out and made his way, as was his custom, to the Mount of Olives; his disciples accompanied him. On reaching the place he said to them, "Pray that you may not be put to the test." He withdrew from them about a stone's throw, then went down on his knees and prayed in these words: "Father, if it is your will, take this cup from me; yet not my will but yours be done." An angel then appeared to him from heaven to strengthen him. In his anguish he prayed with all the greater intensity, and his sweat became like drops of blood falling to the ground. Then he rose from prayer and came to his disciples, only to find them asleep, exhausted with grief. He said to them, "Why are you sleeping? Wake up, and pray that you may not be subjected to the trial."

Meditation: Consider how Mary shares the same sense of sorrow as Jesus, at the sight of so many sins offending God throughout the ages. Have I become blind to sin in myself and in the world, or do I wish to console my God, in union with Mary, mother of Jesus?

- *OUR FATHER, TEN HAIL MARYS, GLORY BE ...*

THE SECOND SORROWFUL MYSTERY

The Scourging at the Pillar
(Mark 15:6–15)

Now on the occasion of a festival Pontius Pilate would release for them one prisoner—any man they asked for. There was a prisoner named Barabbas jailed along with the rebels who had committed murder in the uprising. When the crowd came up to press their demand that he honor the custom, Pilate rejoined, "Do you want me to release the king of the Jews for you?" He was aware, of course, that it was out of jealousy that the chief priests had handed him over. Meanwhile, the chief priests incited the crowd to have him release Barabbas instead. Pilate again asked them, "What am I to do with the man you call the king of the Jews?"

They shouted back, "Crucify him!"

Pilate protested, "Why? What crime has he committed?"

They only shouted the louder, "Crucify him!"

So Pilate, who wished to satisfy the crowd, released Barabbas to them, and after he had had Jesus scourged, he handed him over to be crucified.

Meditation: Consider the sorrow which filled the heart of Mary, seeing her son beaten by the soldiers, and yet the respect she feels at the meekness he displays—a meekness taught to him by her heart. Will I remain as I am, or will I allow myself to be taught by the virtues of the heart of the mother of Our Lord?

- *OUR FATHER, TEN HAIL MARYS, GLORY BE ...*

THE THIRD SORROWFUL MYSTERY

The Crowning with Thorns
(John 19:1–8)

The soldiers then wove a crown of thorns and fixed it on his head, throwing around his shoulders a cloak of royal purple. Repeatedly, they came up to him and said, "All hail, King of the Jews!", slapping his face as they did so.

Pilate went out a second time and said to the crowd: "Observe what I do. I am going to bring him out to you to make you realize that I find no case [against him]." When Jesus came out wearing the crown of thorns and the purple cloak, Pilate said to them, "Look at the man!"

As soon as the chief priests and the temple police saw him they shouted, "Crucify him! Crucify him!"

Pilate said, "Take him and crucify him yourselves; I find no case against him."

"We have our law," the Jews responded, "and according to that law he must die because he made himself God's Son."

When Pilate heard this kind of talk, he was more afraid than ever.

Meditation: Consider the meekness and mercy of the sacred heart of Jesus; do I seek to imitate his virtues or am I stubborn in my sinfulness? Do I implore his mercy for myself and for all souls?

- *Our Father, Ten Hail Marys, Glory Be ...*

The Fourth Sorrowful Mystery

The Carrying of the Cross
(John 19:16–22)

Jesus was led away, and carrying the cross by himself, went out to what is called the Place of the Skull (in Hebrew, Golgotha). There they crucified him, and two others with him: one on either side, Jesus in the middle.

Pilate had an inscription placed on the cross which read, JESUS THE NAZOREAN, THE KING OF THE JEWS. This inscription, in Hebrew, Latin and Greek, was read by many of the Jews, since the place where Jesus was crucified was near the city. The chief priests of the Jews tried to tell Pilate, "You should not have written, 'The King of the Jews.' Write instead, 'This man claimed to be king of the Jews.'"

Pilate answered, "What I have written, I have written."

Meditation: Consider the sad meeting of the hearts of Jesus and Mary on the way to Calvary—a meeting which no words could ever describe.

Do I seek to escape God's will for me, seeking him only when I need his help, or am I able to see the will of God in all the moments of my life, even the most difficult?

- *OUR FATHER, TEN HAIL MARYS, GLORY BE ...*

THE FIFTH SORROWFUL MYSTERY

The Crucifixion and Death of Jesus
(John 19:25–30)

Near the cross of Jesus there stood his mother, his mother's sister, Mary the wife of Clopas, and Mary Magdalene. Seeing his mother there with the disciple whom he loved, Jesus said to his mother, "Woman, there is your son." In turn he said to the disciple, "There is your mother." From that hour onward, the disciple took her into his care. After that, Jesus, realizing that everything was now finished, said to fulfil the Scripture, "I am thirsty." There was a jar there, full of common wine. They stuck a sponge soaked in this wine on some hyssop and raised it to his lips. When Jesus took the wine, he said, "Now it is finished." Then he bowed his head, and delivered over his spirit.

Meditation: Consider Calvary, do I take up my own place on Calvary, uniting myself to Jesus in his passion and death, as did his blessed mother at the foot of the cross?

- *OUR FATHER, TEN HAIL MARYS, GLORY BE ... HAIL HOLY QUEEN*

The Five Glorious Mysteries

THE FIRST GLORIOUS MYSTERY

The Resurrection of Our Lord
(Mark 16:1–7)

When the Sabbath was over, Mary Magdalene, Mary the mother of James, and Salome bought perfumed oils with which they intended to go and anoint Jesus. Very early, just after sunrise, on the first day of the week they came to the tomb. They were saying to one another, "Who will roll back the stone for us from the entrance to the tomb?"

When they looked, they found that the stone had been rolled back. (It was a huge one.) On entering the tomb they saw a young man sitting at the right, dressed in a white robe. This frightened them thoroughly, but he reassured them: "You need not be amazed! You are looking for Jesus of Nazareth, the one who was crucified. He has been raised up; he is not here. See the place where they laid him. Go now and tell his disciples and Peter, 'He is going ahead of you to Galilee, where you will see him just as he told you.'"

Meditation: Consider the immeasurable faith of Mary in the words of her son and in his promise that he would die, but would rise again in three days. Do I seek to question and rationalize my own faith, picking and choosing what to believe and what to reject, or is it as unswaying as the faith of Mary?

- *OUR FATHER, TEN HAIL MARYS, GLORY BE …*

THE SECOND GLORIOUS MYSTERY

The Ascension into Heaven
(Luke 24:46–53)

Jesus said to the Eleven: "Thus it is written that the Messiah must suffer and rise from the dead on the third day. In his name, penance for the remission of sins is to be preached to the nations, beginning at Jerusalem. You are witnesses of this. See, I send down upon you the promise of my father. Remain here in the city until you are clothed with power from on high." He then led them out near Bethany, and with hands upraised, blessed them. As he blessed, he left them, and was taken up into heaven. They fell down to do him reverence, then returned to Jerusalem filled with joy. There they were to be found in the temple constantly, speaking the praises of God.

Meditation: Consider that hope is the opposite of a presumptuous faith; it believes that what has been said is true and will be brought to completion. Mary is the Mother of Fair Hope. Will I try to follow the virtues so perfectly and so humbly displayed by her?

- *OUR FATHER, TEN HAIL MARYS, GLORY BE …*

THE THIRD GLORIOUS MYSTERY

The Descent of the Holy Spirit
(Acts 2:1–7)

When the day of Pentecost came, the disciples were gathered in one place. Suddenly from up in the sky there came a noise like a strong, driving wind which was heard all through the house where they were seated. Tongues as of fire appeared which parted and came to rest on each of them. All were filled with the Holy Spirit. They began to express themselves in foreign tongues and make bold proclamation as the Spirit prompted them. Staying in Jerusalem at the time were devout Jews of every nation under heaven. These heard the sound, and assembled in a large crowd. They were much confused because each one heard these men speaking his own language. The whole occurrence astonished them.

Meditation: Consider how Mary united her own prayers to the prayers of the apostles, asking of God the outpouring of the Holy Spirit upon the Church, as promised by Jesus Christ. Do I criticize the Church and separate myself from it, or do I pray for a new outpouring of the Holy Spirit, to even refresh and remember the Church?

•   *OUR FATHER, TEN HAIL MARYS, GLORY BE …*

THE FOURTH GLORIOUS MYSTERY

The Assumption of Mary into Heaven
(Luke 1:46–55)

Then Mary said: "My being proclaims the greatness of the Lord, my spirit finds joy in God my savior, for he has looked upon his servant in her lowliness; all ages to come shall call me blessed. God who is mighty has done great things for me, holy is his name. His mercy is from age to age on those who fear him. He has shown might with his arm; he has confused the proud in their inmost thoughts. He has deposed the mighty from their thrones and raised the lowly to high places. The hungry he has given every good thing, while the rich he has sent empty away. He has upheld Israel his servant, ever mindful of his mercy; Even as he promised our fathers, promised Abraham and his descendants forever."

Meditation: Consider the life of the Blessed Virgin, and the virtues which were so abundantly found within that life. Seeking God alone in all things, she remained faithful until death, being taken body and soul into Heaven. Am I truly devoted to her God in that same way?

- OUR FATHER, TEN HAIL MARYS, GLORY BE ...

THE FIFTH GLORIOUS MYSTERY

The Coronation of Mary
(Judith 13:18, 19–20)

Blessed are you, daughter, by the Most High God, above all the women on earth; and blessed be the LORD God, the creator of heaven and earth ... Your deed of hope will never be forgotten by those who tell of the might of God. May God make this redound to your everlasting honor, rewarding you with blessings, because you risked your life when your people were being oppressed, and you averted our disaster, walking uprightly before God."

And all the people answered, "Amen! Amen!"

Meditation: Consider the honor paid to the Blessed Virgin in Heaven by the Most Holy Trinity, by whom she is crowned Queen of Heaven and Queen of All Hearts. If this is the honor paid to her by God, can anything less be expected of me?

- OUR FATHER, TEN HAIL MARYS, GLORY BE ...

The Luminous Mysteries

The late Pope John Paul II's Apostolic Letter introduced the Luminous Mysteries in October 2002. Five mysteries, the Mysteries of Light (or the Luminous Mysteries), were added to the rosary. They focus on the public ministry of Jesus Christ.

The Baptism of Jesus in the Jordan
(Matthew 3:13–16)

Here, as Christ descends into the waters, the innocent one who became "sin" for our sake (cf. 2 Corinthians 5:21), the heavens open wide and the voice of the Father declares him the beloved Son (cf. Matthew 3:17), while the Spirit descends on him to invest him with the mission which he is to carry out..

Meditation: Heavenly Father, as we offer you this mystery, we pray for the grace of a deeper conversion. In our baptism, we have received the light of Christ in our hearts, may his grace renew us constantly and reach also all those who have not been baptized and don't know him. The Holy Trinity was present in this mystery, as a sign of the joy of God for all his children being baptized and becoming members of the body of Christ.

With St John the Baptist, let us be transformed by saying, "I must decrease so that the Lord may increase."

- *Our Father, Ten Hail Marys, Glory Be …*

The Wedding at Cana
(John 2:1–12)

The first of the signs, given at Cana (cf. John 2:1–12), is when Christ changes water into wine and opens the hearts of the disciples to faith, thanks to the intervention of Mary, the first among believers.

Meditation: Heavenly Father, as we offer you this mystery, we pray in thanksgiving for revealing your power through your Son, Our Lord Jesus Christ. Just as Jesus transformed water into wine, we pray that we may be transformed by your light through the intercession of the Blessed Virgin Mary. Mary said to Jesus, "They have no wine." The Lord responded by performing his first miracle. When we put our faith in the intercession of our Heavenly Mother, we have a sure way of receiving miraculously from the Lord.

We pray also in this mystery for a blessing upon all families since Jesus and Mary are so pleased in the holy sacrament of marriage.

- *OUR FATHER, TEN HAIL MARYS, GLORY BE …*

THE THIRD LUMINOUS MYSTERY
The Proclamation of the Kingdom
(Mark 1:14–15)

The preaching by which Jesus proclaims the coming of the Kingdom of God, calls us to conversion (cf. Mk 1:15) and forgives the sins of all who draw near to him in humble trust (cf. Mk 2:3–13; Lk 7:47–48): and it tells out the inauguration of that ministry of mercy which he continues to exercise until the end of the world, particularly through the Sacrament of Reconciliation which he has entrusted to his Church (cf. Jn 20:22–23).

Meditation: Heavenly Father, as we offer you this mystery, we open our hearts to the teachings of your Son, Jesus Christ, the incarnate Word of God. We come in our darkness to be filled with the light of Christ who says, "I am the light of the world."

We come in our emptiness to be filled with his wisdom. We confess our sinfulness and pray for the grace of being transformed by his words and become holy.

- *OUR FATHER, TEN HAIL MARYS, GLORY BE …*

THE FOURTH LUMINOUS MYSTERY
The Transfiguration
(Matthew 17:1–8)

The mystery of light par excellence is the Transfiguration, traditionally believed to have taken place on Mount Tabor. The glory of the Godhead shines forth from the face of Christ as the Father commands the astonished Apostles to "listen to him" (cf. Lk 9:35 and parallels) and to prepare to experience with him the agony of the Passion, so as to come with him to the joy of the Resurrection and a life transfigured by the Holy Spirit.

Meditation: Heavenly Father, as we offer you this mystery, we pray that the light of Christ will transform our lives, raising us from the dust of our human existence into the light of the divinity. We strive to live a holy life and aspire to say with St. Paul, "It is no longer I who live, but

Christ who lives in me." With St. Peter, we rejoice in the spiritual life and say, "Lord, it is good to be here."

- *OUR FATHER, TEN HAIL MARYS, GLORY BE ...*

THE FIFTH LUMINOUS MYSTERY

The Institution of the Eucharist
(Matthew 26)

Christ offers his body and blood as food under the signs of bread and wine, and testifies "to the end" his love for humanity (John 13:1), for whose salvation he will offer himself in sacrifice.

Meditation: Heavenly Father, as we offer you this mystery, we thank you for providing us with our daily spiritual bread, the light of our souls. We pray that you will give us hunger for the Holy Eucharist and the highest reverence for the presence of your Son, Emmanuel, the Bread of Life, God with us in the Sacrifice of the Holy Mass.

We pray for adoration of the Blessed Sacrament, the Eucharistic presence of Jesus: flesh, blood, soul, and divinity in the consecrated bread and wine. We pray for all priests to be made holy, for the worthy reception of this holy Sacrament by the preparation of the faithful with a good confession. We pray for the spread of your Eucharistic kingdom throughout the world to transform the children of Adam into the children of God.

- *OUR FATHER, TEN HAIL MARYS, GLORY BE ...*

The Liturgy of the Hours and the Divine Office

As you begin to develop in prayer, you may wish to begin to pray the Divine Office or Liturgy of the Hours. You will see that this is something to grow into, not to be taken on early in the development of your prayer life.

There are many variations on the Divine Office, but one thing is important to remember: If you are struggling with simple daily prayer at one or two points of the day, taking on even the basic aspects of these prayers and readings inevitably leads to disappointment and may cause harm to your new prayer life.

Work your way up to these devotions slowly, using regular morning and evening prayer as the "baseline" for establishing regular prayers and then slowly adding in these other "offices" of the day.

WHAT IS THE DIVINE OFFICE OR LITURGY OF THE HOURS?

The Liturgy of the Hours is the liturgical embodiment of the canonical hours of the Church and are prayed, under various names, by both Eastern and Western Catholics, Anglicans, Orthodox, Oriental, and Coptic churches.

Liturgy of the Hours is the name used for the Divine Office of the Latin Rite of the Roman Catholic Church after the reforms of the Second Vatican Council. The American English translation uses the name Liturgy of the Hours; the most popular Commonwealth English translation retains the name Divine Office. For traditional Anglicans, the Book of Common Prayer (1928 or 1662) includes a simplified version, distilled to morning and evening prayer.

Some religious orders have their own versions of the Divine Office, including the Benedictines and Carthusians, and do not use the typical edition of the Liturgy of the Hours. The liturgy is included in prayer books called breviaries and some devotional guides in simplified form.

The Code of Canon Law of the Roman Catholic Church says of the Liturgy of the Hours:

In the Liturgy of the Hours, the Church, hearing God speaking to his people and recalling the mystery of salvation, praises him without ceasing by song and prayer and intercedes for the salvation of the whole world.

At prescribed times throughout the day, psalms and prayers from the Psalter are recited or sung privately, in common, or in choir. The Liturgy of the Hours is most common among the clergy and religious orders; ordained clergy are required by canon law to pray the Liturgy of the Hours, while members of religious orders are bound by the constitution of their order. The Christian faithful have been urged to take up the practice, and as a result, many lay people have begun reciting portions of the Liturgy of the Hours.

TRADITIONAL HOURS

In the Roman Catholic Church, the Liturgy of the Hours has undergone a vast transformation since the Second Vatican Council. Although among religious orders, traditional Anglicans and others, the Liturgy has kept the eight "hours" (or offices) be said by the secular clergy and religious each day. This was itself following St. Benedict's Rule, which laid down the following offices:

- Matins (during the night)
- Lauds or Morning Prayer (at dawn)
- Prime or Early Morning Prayer (the First Hour = 6:00 am)
- Terce or Mid-morning Prayer (the Third Hour = 9:00 am)
- Sext or Midday Prayer (the Sixth Hour = 12:00 pm)
- None or Mid-afternoon Prayer (the Ninth Hour = 3:00 pm)
- Vespers or Evening Prayer (at the lighting of the lamps)
- Compline or Night Prayer (before retiring)

Matins is nocturnal in character, as witnessed by the "rising out of sleep" theme of many of the hymns sung at that hour. The design of this scheme of prayer was to be in fulfillment of the scriptures: "Seven times a day do I praise you" (Psalm 119:164) and "In the middle of the night I arose to glorify You" (Psalm 119:62).

The structure of the hours was varied, but balanced. Matins (the longest hour) began with the words, "Lord, open thou my lips, and my mouth shall show forth your praise," followed by an antiphon and the Invitatory Psalm: Psalm 94 from the Vulgate and Septuagint—which is equivalent to Psalm 95 in the Hebrew—"Venite exultemus Domino," meaning "Come, let us sing to the Lord." This was then followed by a hymn and three "Nocturns" consisting of three psalms each, with lessons from scripture and concerning the saint celebrated on the day.

For major festivals, the ninth (and final) lesson was concluded by the singing of "Te Deum," an ancient hymn of thanksgiving to God dating possibly from St. Ambrose of Milan.

Lauds and vespers share a similar structure, consisting of the Opening Versicles (O God, make speed to save us etc.), followed by four psalms and a canticle (from the Old Testament) at lauds, and, at vespers, five psalms, with antiphons. These are followed by a *capitulum* or "little chapter" from scripture, a hymn, and a brief response to the chapter. There then follows the singing of the *Benedictus* at lauds, or the *Magnificat* at vespers. These are the great New Testament canticles of God's salvation. On some days, there followed *preces* or prayers, and then the office concluded.

Terce, sext, and none had identical structure. They began with the opening versicles and a hymn, followed by three psalms with antiphons. There followed a capitulum and response, followed by the Lesser Litany (Kyrie and the Lord's Prayer), followed by the conclusion of the office.

Prime and Compline also shared highly similar structures, which were yet different from that of terce, sext, and none (the other "little" offices).

This older liturgy is by no means obsolete, with some religious orders and many lay people continuing to use this system in their daily prayer.

MODERN PRACTICE

The Second Vatican Council introduced a widespread reform of the Liturgy of the Hours (as it was thereafter designated). While this is distinctly different from what preceded it, it is in no way less balanced or ordered. In addition, many of the complicated Rubrics (or instructions) printed in Breviarium Romanum (the Breviary) were simplified, so that the actual method of praying the office became simpler. In many ways, the forms are similar to the morning and evening prayer offices in the Book of Common Prayer. The General Instruction of the Liturgy of the Hours designates the following hours as currently required of all Roman Catholic clergy and recommended to all Roman Catholics (other folks can use them, too!).

- Invitatory (*Invitatorium*): This is not an hour properly called, but the introduction to the first hour said on the current day, whether the Office of Readings or morning prayer.

- Office of Readings or Matins/Vigils (*Officium Lectionis*): This hour may be prayed any time during the day, but preferably in the nocturnal hours for religious in choir.

- Morning Prayer or Lauds (*Laudes Matutinae*): This hour is prayed at sunrise or in the early morning.

- Daytime Prayer (*Hora Media*): This hour consists of one or more of the following, depending on the time of day it is said:

- Mid-morning Prayer or Terce (Tertia)
- Midday Prayer or Sext (Sexta)
- Mid-afternoon Prayer or None (Nona).
- <u>Evening Prayer</u> or Vespers (*Vesperae*): This is prayed in the evening, around six o'clock or sunset.
- <u>Night Prayer</u> or Compline (*Completorium*): This hour is prayed before retiring.

Traditionally, all 150 psalms were said during the course of a week. In the 1971 and 2000 editions of the Breviarium Romanum, 148 psalms (excluding two imprecatory psalms and some verses of others) are said during a four-week cycle. The Psalterium Monasticum (1981) arranges all 150 psalms plus the canticles into a one-week cycle for optional use in the new liturgy.

You can learn more about the Liturgy of the Hours and how to keep them online at the following Web sites:

Traditional Hours (with Latin)
Confraternity of Ss. Peter and Paul
http://www.breviary.net/

Anglican Traditional Hours
Anglican Breviary
http://www.anglicanbreviary.com/

Modern Liturgy of the Hours
Liturgy of the Hours Apostolate
http://www.liturgyhours.org/

Universalis
http://www.universalis.com/

Benedictine
Multiple sources and breviaries
http://www.osb.org/liturgy/

The Simplest Prayer

As writer Peter Kreeft points out, the simplest prayer in the world is "Jesus." There is power in his name and healing and comfort and boundless love.

Just to call upon him means that the conversation has started, and you are praying.

✠

APPENDIX

SUGGESTED READING AND RESOURCES

This list is by no means exhaustive and is representative of the author's preferences and favorites. If there is something you would like to see added in future editions, please contact the author at cnalls@canonlaw.org

God bless, and please, pray for me as I pray for you.

LITURGY OF THE HOURS
Liturgy of the Hours, (Leather Bound)(Four Volumes), Catholic Book Publishing Company (July 1999), ISBN-10: 0899424112.

Christian Prayer: The Liturgy of the Hours, (Leather Bound) (One Volume) Catholic Book Publishing Company (Book & Guide edition) (December 1999), ISBN-10: 0899424066.

Anglican Breviary (reprint of the Frank Gavin Liturgical Foundation Edition, 1955) available from http://www.anglicanbreviary.com/ordering.html

The Monastic Diurnal or Day Hours of the Monastic Breviary, According to the Holy Rule of Saint Benedict in Latin and English, (Leather Bound), Farnborough Abbey (2004), ISBN-10: 0907077447.

Daily Prayer from the Divine Office: The Liturgy of the Hours According to the Roman Rite, Collins (1974), ISBN-10: 0059950403.

PRAYER BOOKS

The 1928 Book of Common Prayer, Oxford University Press, USA (November 18, 1993), ISBN-10: 0195285069.

The 1662 Book of Common Prayer, Oxford University Press, USA (May 1, 2001), ISBN-10: 0191306010.

1928 Book of Common Prayer with Authorized King James Bible and Apocrypha, Preservation Press (1995), ISBN-10: 1886412022, now available from the Anglican Parishes Association, http://www.anglicanbooks. com/

Saint Benedict's Prayer Book for Beginners (Hardcover), Ampleforth Abbey Press Gracewing (June 1994), ISBN-10: 0852442580.

Fulton Sheen's Wartime Prayer Book, Fulton J. Sheen, Sophia Institute Press (2003), ISBN-10: 1928832652.

VARIOUS BOOKS ON PRAYER AND THE SPIRITUAL LIFE
Praying in the Presence of Our Lord with Fulton J. Sheen, Fulton Sheen, Michael Dubruiel, Benedict Groeschel, Our Sunday Visitor (March 1, 2002), ISBN-10: 0879737158.

The Practice of the Presence of God: With Spiritual Maxims, Brother Lawrence Publisher: Revell, Reprint edition (January 1999), ISBN-10: 0800785991.

The School of Prayer: An Introduction to the Divine Office for All Christians (Turtleback), John Brook, Liturgical Press (December 1991), ISBN-10: 0814620280.

The Divine Office for Dodos: A Step-by-Step Guide to Praying the Liturgy of the Hours (Paperback), Madeline Pecora Nugent, Three Bean Books (May 1, 2004), ISBN-10: 0974464406.

Abandonment to Divine Providence, Jean-Pierre de Caussade Publisher: Cosimo Classics (April 15, 2007), ISBN-10: 1602064334.

Trustful Surrender to Divine Providence: The Secret to Peace and Happiness, Jean Baptiste Saint-Jure, Saint Claude de la Colombière, Tan Books & Publishers (June 1983), ISBN-10: 0895552167.

The Spiritual Direction of Saint Claude de la Colombière, Saint Claude de la Colombière and Mary Philip, Ignatius Press, Reprint edition (February 1998), ISBN-10: 0898706823.

The Spiritual Combat, and a Treatise on Peace of the Soul, Dom. Lorenzo Scupoli, Tan Books & Publishers (December 1990), ISBN-10: 0895554054.

Dark Night of the Soul: A Masterpiece in the Literature of Mysticism by St. John of the Cross, Image, Reprint edition (January 11, 1959), ISBN-10: 0385029306.

The Spiritual Exercises of St. Ignatius, St. Ignatius, Image, Reissue edition (January 7, 1964), ISBN-10: 0385024363.

Introduction to the Devout Life, St. Francis De Sales, Vintage, 1st edition (April 9, 2002) ISBN-10: 0375725628.

The Way of Perfection, St. Theresa of Avila, Paraclete Press (MA) (April 2000), ISBN-10: 1557252483.

Interior Castle, St. Teresa of Avila, Image, Reissue edition, (January 4, 1972), ISBN-10: 0385036434.

Finding God's Will for You, St. Francis de Sales, Sophia Institute Press (October 1998), ISBN-10: 0918477832.

The Prayers and Meditations of Saint Anselm, St. Anselm, Penguin Classics, Reprint edition (November 29, 1979), ISBN-10: 0140442782.

The Art of Praying: The Principles and Methods of Christian Prayer (formerly entitled *Prayer in Practice*), Romano Guardini, Sophia Institute Press (October 1995), ISBN-10: 0918477344.

The Aquinas Prayer Book: The Prayers and Hymns of St. Thomas Aquinas, Robert Anderson and Johannes Moser, Sophia Institute Press, New (September 2000), ISBN-10: 1928832148.

The Rosary: Chain of Hope, Benedict Groeschel, Ignatius Press (June 2003), ISBN-10: 0898709830.

The Benedictine Handbook, Anthony Marett-Crosby Liturgical Press (August 2003), ISBN-10: 0814627900.

The Riches of the Rosary, Gabriel Harty, Veritas Books (August 1997), ISBN-10: 1853903671.

The Lord's Prayer, Romano Guardini, Sophia Institute Press (October 1996), ISBN-10: 0918477468.

Praying in the Presence of Our Lord: With St. Thomas Aquinas (Praying in the Presence), Mike Aquilina, Our Sunday Visitor (March 2002), ISBN-10: 0879739584.

The Rosary of Our Lady, Romano Guardini Sophia Institute Press (October 1998), ISBN-10: 0918477786.

www.ingramcontent.com/pod-product-compliance
Lightning Source LLC
Chambersburg PA
CBHW032026040426
42448CB00006B/735